A WORLD OF HOLIDAYS

CARNIVAL

A WORLD OF HOLIDAYS

CARNIVAL

Catherine Chambers

RSVP
RAINTREE
STECK-VAUGHN
PUBLISHERS
The Steck-Vaughn Company
Austin, Texas

Published by Raintree Steck-Vaughn Publishers, an imprint of Steck-Vaughn Company

Library of Congress Cataloging-in-Publication Data

Chambers, Catherine.
    Carnival / Catherine Chambers.
        p.   cm. — (A world of holidays)
    Includes bibliographical references and index.
    Summary: Introduces the holiday of Carnival and explains how it is celebrated all over the world.
    ISBN 0-8172-4613-4
    1. Carnival—Juvenile literature.   [1. Carnival.
2. Holidays.]   I. Title.   II. Series.
GT4180.C48   1998
394.25—dc21   97-18329
                                                CIP
                                                AC

Printed in Spain
Bound in United States
1 2 3 4 5 6 7 8 9 0 01 00 99 98 97

ACKNOWLEDGMENTS

Editors: Su Swallow, Pam Wells
Design: TJ Graphics
Production: Jenny Mulvanny
Picture research: Victoria Brooker

The publishers would like to thank the Reverend Martin J. Burne, O.S.B., Saint Mary's Abbey, Morristown, New Jersey, for reading and advising on the manuscript.

For permission to reproduce copyright material, the author and publishers gratefully acknowledge the following:

cover: Zefa Pictures
title page: Sylvain Grandadam/Tony Stone Images
page 6 Oliver Benn, Tony Stone Images **page 7** (top) Sue Cunningham (bottom) Ian Murphy/Tony Stone Images **page 8** Beresford Hills/Sylvia Cordaiy Photo Library **page 9** (top) Trip/H Gariety (bottom) Hutchison Library **page 10** Travel Ink/Ronald Badkin **page 11** (left) Zefa Pictures (right) Travel Ink/Andrew Cowin **page 12** Mick Csaky/Hutchison Library **page 13** (top) Bruno De Hogues/Tony Stone Images (bottom) Sylvain Grandadam/Tony Stone Images **page 14** Sue Cunningham **page 15** (top) Jean-Leo Dugast/Panos Pictures (bottom) Travel Ink/Peter Murphy **page 16** Philip Wolmuth/Hutchison Library **page 17** (top) Travel Ink/Peter Murphy (bottom) Cees van Leeuwen/Sylvia Cordaiy Photo Library **page 18** Randy Wells/Tony Stone Images **page 19** A Boccaccio/Image Bank **page 20** Zefa Pictures **page 21** (top) Travel Ink/Nick Battersby (bottom) Trip/Viesti Associates **page 22** Sue Cunningham **page 23** (left) Sue Cunningham Photographic (right) Trip/H Rogers **page 24** Jean-Leo Dugast/Panos Pictures **page 25** (top) Zefa Pictures (bottom) Trip/F Andreescu **page 26** Travel Ink/Andrew Cowin **page 27** (top) Guildhall Art Gallery, Corporation of London/Bridgeman Art Library (bottom) CIRCA Photo Library/©John Fryer **page 28 and 29** Alan Towse

Contents

What Is Carnival?

Carnival is a holiday of dazzling color and throbbing music. It seems to have a life of its own. But it began with a serious Christian holiday.

A REAL PROBLEM

Christians follow the teachings of Jesus Christ. There are many holidays in the year that remind Christians of the life of Jesus. Of course, Christmas marks Jesus' birth. Carnival marks the time before Lent. This is the time of the year when Christians remember how God gave Jesus a difficult test. Jesus went into the desert for 40 days. Here, he had to fight with the devil. He had to decide if he should go out and teach about God's love and forgiveness. It seems an easy decision to make. But Jesus knew that his ideas would make some people angry. He knew that in the end it would lead to his death.

In Trinidad, a child parades in a bird costume with feathers like flames. Children often have their own Carnival parade.

THE MEANING OF CARNIVAL

The most important day of Carnival is Shrove Tuesday, the day right before Lent. In the past on this day, Christians confessed their sins and received forgiveness. "Carnival" means "doing without meat." It reminds people of the old custom

6

of fasting for 40 days. This is the time Jesus spent in the desert — the time of Lent.

People once gave up all rich foods for Lent. Today, they don't fast as much. Children often give up something they really like at Lent — like chocolate or soft drinks. But they are also often asked to spend some of their free time helping other people. This is a very useful and thoughtful thing to do.

Just before the difficult time of Lent, comes a time for really letting go! From Europe to the Americas, Carnival is celebrated with parades, bright costumes, music, and good food.

▲ Food sellers in booths make sure that no one gets hungry during Carnival.

◀ In the Italian city of Venice, a mysterious woman parades in a golden mask.

The Wilderness

In the hustle and bustle of Carnival it is easy to forget about Lent — the time Jesus spent in the wilderness.

FIGHTING WITH THE DEVIL

Jesus Christ knew that he had to serve God. But he also knew that it would be a very tough task. He knew that God would test him.

God sent a Spirit to lead Jesus into the desert. There, Jesus stayed for 40 days and 40 nights. He had no food to eat. By the end of that time Jesus was weak and desperately hungry. So the devil came to him and said, "So you think you're the Son of God, do you? Well then, turn some of these stones into bread to prove it!" But Jesus shook his head and refused to do a trick for the devil, even though he was starving.

Then, the devil took Jesus up to the top of a temple in Jerusalem and said, "If you really are the Son of God, throw yourself off this temple. Go on, your angels will stop you from hitting the ground, won't they?" But again Jesus refused to do as the devil wanted.

Christ fasted in an empty wilderness like this one in Jordan, a country in the Middle East.

Finally, the devil took Jesus to the top of a very high mountain. He showed Jesus all the kingdoms in the world. "Now listen," he said. "I will give you *all this*. But you must first kneel at my feet and worship me." But Jesus was much stronger than the devil. "You'd better get out of my way," said Jesus. "There is only one God, and I will worship him and serve him, not you." So the devil disappeared, and angels came to give Jesus food and drink.

Jesus knew that he now had to prove his love of God to the rest of the world. He had to teach others about God's love and forgiveness. Then he had to die and take with him the sins of the world.

Jesus then spread his teachings around Galilee in Palestine — his followers, the apostles, by his side.

Jesus is surrounded by his closest followers, the apostles, in this stained-glass window.

This is the Sea of Galilee, where Christ spread his teachings.

One Last Fling!

It's almost time to give up some of the treats you really like. So you'd better have one last fling!

FIRST THE FUN—THEN THE FAST

The leaders of the Christian Church knew just how difficult Lent was. Fasting and confessing are not easy things to do. So they let Christians have one last fling before the hard times ahead. This became known as Carnival.

Ancient early spring celebrations held in Europe became an important part of this holiday. In France, one of these traditions was to lead a fattened cow through the streets. Behind came a procession of people dressed in colorful, fancy costumes.

When Christianity came, the spring parade brightened the towns and villages on the last day before Lent. In France and in New Orleans,

These old buildings in New Orleans show how the French brought their traditions to North America. Carnival was one of these traditions.

this day is called "Mardi Gras," which means "Fat Tuesday." Everyone on this day used up all their rich foods, including fats such as butter. This left people with only simple foods to eat during the fast. But it was the parade and costumes that became the heart of Carnival as we know it today.

Parades, processions, costumes, and music are all part of the fun.

Europeans brought Carnival to these Caribbean islands. They also brought Africans, who made Caribbean Carnival what it is today.

ACROSS THE OCEAN

How did Carnival become such a huge festival? Well, about 300 years ago, European explorers crossed the Atlantic Ocean. They landed on the shores of North and South America and on islands in the Caribbean Sea.

European governments took over these parts of the lands. Later, other European settlers came to set up farms and businesses. They brought their customs and traditions with them. One of them was Carnival.

 # Out of Africa

In North and South America, Carnival is now a brilliant show of music, dance, and dazzling costumes. Africans who were taken to the Americas helped make Carnival exciting.

A EUROPEAN HOLIDAY

At first, European settlers in the Americas and the Caribbean celebrated Carnival as they had done back home. But the festival, or holiday, slowly began to change. It took on African culture and customs, too.

African slaves were brought to the Americas and the islands of the Caribbean for over 300 years. They were forced to work in terrible conditions for their European masters. Africans were not allowed to take part in festivals. But in Carnival processions, some of the slave owners began to dress as their African slaves did — just for the day.

Changing places with servants and slaves for a day is a very old tradition in Europe. The ancient Romans did it during the festival of Saturnalia. So did the English in their Feast of Fools, hundreds of years ago.

These costumes are being worn by the Dogon people of West Africa. Many Carnival costumes are based on African festival dress.

A FESTIVAL OF FREEDOM

When slaves finally became free over 100 years ago, the holiday changed even more. The custom of changing places with slaves had been mocking and cruel. So instead, Africans began to join in the Carnival.

At first, Africans paraded in their best clothes. These were like the clothes of the Europeans. But

A lot of Carnival drumming comes from African rhythms. Here in Burundi, in Central Africa, drummers are playing during a festival.

gradually, they began to dress as if they were characters from African stories. Processions burst with bright costumes — from huge feathered birds to spirits of fire. The cities of Rio de Janeiro, in South America, and New Orleans, Louisiana, became centers for the new Carnival. And on the islands of the Caribbean, the holiday became a joyful celebration of freedom.

The colors and shapes of Carnival headdresses can be found in African festival head coverings. But Carnival makes them even brighter and bigger!

13

Let's Get Ready!

It takes a long time to get ready for Carnival. Some people start soon after the last one has ended!

AN EARLY START— STAGE ONE

After the dizzy days of Carnival in the Americas, everyone's exhausted. But after a month or two they start thinking about next year's show. First, the groups get together.

In New Orleans, Louisiana, some of the groups are over 150 years old. In Brazil, Samba dance schools take part in Carnival. Workers' organizations and local residents' groups join in, too.

WHAT SHALL WE DO?— STAGE TWO

The groups have to choose a theme for their procession. The costumes all have to follow the theme. Some groups choose characters from a story. Others might stay with traditional costumes from long ago.

LET'S GET GOING— STAGE THREE

Colors and designs are chosen. Materials are bought — wire, light wood, plastics, and metals are used for the frames. Silks, satins, velvet, paper, and metallic fabric cover them. Sequins, beads, and feathers are common decorations. For the rich groups, money is spent freely on the costumes. The poor have to scrimp and save. But their displays are just as spectacular.

The final decorations are being put together for the Rio Carnival. People work late into the night to make everything perfect.

14

In Sardinia, musicians make sure they look sharp for Carnival.

THE EXCITEMENT BEGINS — STAGE FOUR

It's just after Christmas. Everything is quiet. But in Brazil, the silence is broken by soft drumming. Children run along the streets playing tin whistles. As New Year is forgotten, and the Carnival month of February gets closer, the music gets louder. In New Orleans, the rich give lavish parties. In gorgeous gowns, people dance into the night.

Are all the flowers on right? These women in the Canary Islands are just checking.

15

"Come on, Take Me to the Mardi Gras!"

Banners of playing cards sway among the masked dancers in Trinidad.

Night and day, Carnival blazes through the streets. Which is the most fantastic costume — or the best band? Here are just a few Carnival snapshots.

CARIBBEAN CARNIVAL

"Jouvé! Daybreak!" That's what islanders of Trinidad and Tobago shout as the first of the two big days of the Carnival begin. It's time for frenzied dancing and throbbing music — together known as "jump-up." At 4 AM on Carnival Monday, the *mas*, or masquerade begins. Music is at the heart of *mas*. The players swarm onto the streets, smeared with oil, mud, or . . . chocolate sauce! Bands play into the night and throughout the following day. But which is the best band? There are judges to crown whoever wins.

What else can you see? Huge trucks, 30 feet (10 m) tall, carry towers of speakers. They blast out the music. Then a sea of dazzling costumes hits the streets. First come the imps led by a huge devil with glistening eyes and a wicked smile. The groups follow, each with a king, a queen, and royal officials. But anyone can join in.

16

You'll see clowns and jesters dancing along as they have done for hundreds of years. Figures from ancient times parade past — from Aztecs and Egyptians to Romans and Vikings. Characters from African folktales act out their story for the crowds.

But what's this coming now? Incredible costumes that no one has ever seen before. You might recognize some of them — the birds of paradise or Neptune, the king of the sea. But many are just out of this world!

What an amazing bird! He is "flying" along the streets of Aruba in the Antilles.

Clowns get ready for their parade in the Canary Islands. Clowns are a traditional part of Carnival.

So who made the finest costume? The Carnival judges make their choices. And then the processions and the bands continue through the following day.

17

You don't have to dress up to join in New Orleans' Carnival. Tourists flock to the city during Carnival time.

DOWN IN NEW ORLEANS

For more than two weeks before Mardi Gras, huge decorated floats lumber along the city streets. But who are the people on them? No one knows — because they all have to wear masks.

The Monday before Carnival is now known as Lundi Gras — or Fat Monday. On this day, Rex, the king of Carnival, is carried along the river in a boat. With music and fireworks he reaches the city. He is ready to start his reign as king.

On Mardi Gras, the parade of Rex is the most important. But the Mardi Gras Indian groups dazzle the spectators. Each group has a Big Chief who is dressed in a huge, brightly-colored costume. Each is covered in patterns made of thousands of tiny beads or shiny sequins. The Mardi Gras Indians are, in fact, from the city's African American communities. Their Carnival music, dancing, and chanting are echoes of their African past.

Carnival in New Orleans dies at midnight on Mardi Gras.

SOUTH AMERICAN STYLE

Close to Carnival, people parade through the streets beating drums, blowing whistles, and ringing triangles. They make yelping calls known as *cuica*. Then the great day arrives. The displays are perfect. Some of the groups have hundreds of people in them. They are all dressed the same and dance in precise rhythm.

In Recife, a port in Brazil, the Carnival lasts for ten days. One of the greatest attractions is the Maracuta. These are performers dressed in African costumes. They act out plays about the kings and queens of Congo in Central Africa.

In Rio, a procession of brightly dressed horses leads a dazzling decorated float. Can you guess what theme they are showing?

 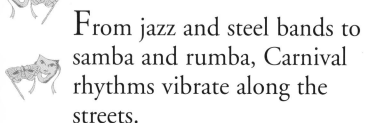 # Dance to the Music!

From jazz and steel bands to samba and rumba, Carnival rhythms vibrate along the streets.

FROM TROMBONES TO COMBS

The jazz bands of New Orleans can make you deaf! Jazz is the favorite Carnival music in the South. Many of its sounds and rhythms come from Africa — its instruments mainly from Europe.

The Mardi Gras Indians have given New Orleans' Carnival a very special type of music. Like jazz, it certainly has African sounds. But the instruments are very different. There are no trumpets or trombones. The musicians use bottles, combs, sticks, drums, and tambourines. The leaders of the band sing out a line of song. Then the rest of the singers sing back a reply. This type of song is called "call-and-response."

Jazz is the heart of music in New Orleans. During Carnival it is played in bars, clubs, and on the street, too.

DANCE FOR THE GODS!

Candomblé groups dance down the streets of Salvador in Brazil. They wear African costume. Candomblé is a religion. It means "dance," for singing and dancing are important for making contact with the gods. But a different type of music blasts from the backs of trucks. It is from the *trios electricos* groups with their modern electronic South American sound.

Along with samba and rumba rhythms and dances of Recife and Olinda comes the Urso. Urso means "bear," and the dances are about the hunting and the training of bears.

On the islands of the Caribbean, the traditional sounds of calypso can still be heard. Wonderful steel bands play every tune under the sun. But *soca* bands are now the fashion. A mixture of soul and calypso, it is great to hear!

▲ In Rio, dancers put on a samba show with full Carnival costume.

▶ In Grenada, in the Caribbean, steel bands entertain the Carnival crowds.

Cooking for Carnival

In New Orleans, Carnival, or Mardi Gras, season begins with King Cake. And stands of favorite foods line the holiday streets.

During Carnival, you'll find plenty of food sellers along the streets of the Brazilian city of Salvador.

KING CAKES — AND WOODEN CAKES!

It is Epiphany — the end of Christmas. This is the time when Christians celebrate the journey of the Three Kings to Bethlehem. They had come to greet the newborn baby Jesus. But according to old French traditions, it is also the start of the Carnival season.

So the ancient Epiphany King Cake has also become Carnival cake. It is flat and baked in the shape of a rectangle. Some are covered in icing and colored sugar. Inside, you'll find a surprise — maybe a tiny plastic baby, but more often, a bean!

King cakes are eaten at Carnival parties and in offices. At the grand ball of the Twelfth Night Revelers, in New Orleans, King cake is very special. The girl who chooses the slice with the golden bean in it becomes the next Carnival queen. Girls are also offered slices of . . . a wooden cake!

PILES OF PANCAKES

For hundreds of years, people in parts of Europe made pancakes on Shrove Tuesday. They used up their fat, eggs, and flour before the fast of Lent. New England pancakes are made with cream, lots of eggs, and a sprinkle of sugar and cinnamon. Some people toss pancakes up in the air and try to catch them in the frying pan. Other people race with them!

A pile of pancakes waiting for their tasty fillings!

FESTIVAL FEASTS

Dancing through the streets at Carnival can make you very hungry. But there's plenty of the local favorite food to eat. In the Caribbean you will find stands of tasty fried, spiced chicken. In Brazil you might eat lucky *bahia* dishes — seafood cooked in oil with coconut milk, cashew nuts, peanuts, and spices.

You can grab a handful of nuts as you pass by this stand during Carnival in Brazil!

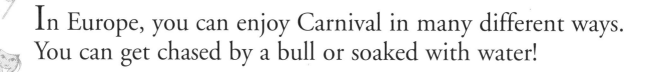 # Other Antics!

In Europe, you can enjoy Carnival in many different ways. You can get chased by a bull or soaked with water!

LET'S BURY THE DEVIL!

If you look back at the story of Lent, you will see that in the end Jesus chased the devil away. Well, in the Spanish town of Villanueva de la Frontera, people make a model of the devil. On the night of Carnival, they carry the devil through the streets. Then they toss him around, cut his head off, and bury him!

Things are even more dangerous in Ciudad Rodrigo. Bulls are let loose on the streets. Young men try to face them. Others just run for safety, screaming as they go!

In Sardinia for the last 400 years, a Carnival tradition called Sartiglia has taken place. Masked horsemen try to pierce metal stars with their swords as they gallop down the street.

MORE MASQUERADES

In Tuscany, Carnival has parades a little like those in the Americas. But the processions are full of humor. The traditional costumes are of

Masked riders get ready for the *Sartiglia* challenge in Sardinia.

Epiphany marks the beginning of Carnival in many parts of Europe, just as it does in the Americas. On this day in Portugal, children run around squirting each other with squirt guns. And the weather's really cold, too!

The best Carnival scenes in Portugal are in the ancient town of Loulé. Besides parades, lots of market stands are set up. In Loulé fairs are a big part of the religious holidays.

On the eve of Lent, masqueraders parade the streets of Germany.

Carnival capers in Bucharest, in Romania.

harlequins, royal courtiers, jesters, ... and popes! Funny scenes are set up on the floats. People make fun of others from behind their masks. Some of the jokes are aimed at politicians or religious leaders. So it's a good thing that no one can see who's telling the jokes!

The Carnival Is Over

It's time to clear up all the mess. Then Christians can rest and think about the serious season of Lent.

CARNIVAL MUST REST

It's Ash Wednesday — the day after Carnival. The streets are silent. Litter and streamers flutter in the wind. But there's still one more job to do before the mess is cleared up. In parts of the Caribbean and the Americas, a straw model is made. It represents the spirit of Carnival. To mark the end of the season and the beginning of Lent, the model is buried.

CROSSES OF ASHES

The next part of Jesus' story shows us why the first day of Lent is called Ash Wednesday. When Jesus had triumphed over the devil, he faced a different challenge. He had to go out and teach others about God. There were plenty of religious leaders around at that time. But Jesus had something new to say. It was that God loves and forgives all those who want to believe in him.

A lonely figure in Carnival costume, at the end of the festival in Venice, Italy.

26

This painting shows Jesus in the wilderness, where he fasted and struggled with the devil.

Jesus chose some people to go with him while he taught. These were the disciples. Later, they became teachers, too. After a while, Jesus and his disciples had many followers in Palestine.

One day Jesus rode into Jerusalem on a donkey. People cheered and waved palms as he went by. This day is now known as Palm Sunday. Christians still wave palms in church or parade through the streets with them. Some make crosses out of pieces of palm. The crosses and palm leaves are kept until the next year — until Ash Wednesday.

In some churches the palms and crosses are burned to ashes on Ash Wednesday. Then, the ashes are used to mark a cross on the foreheads of churchgoers. On this day, the color of Carnival is quickly forgotten. But it isn't long before the next Carnival is being planned!

On Ash Wednesday, an ash cross is marked on this girl's forehead.

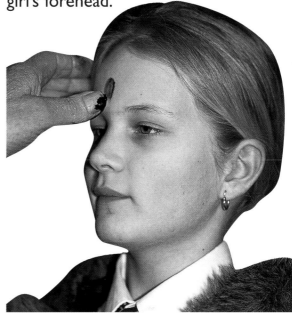

27

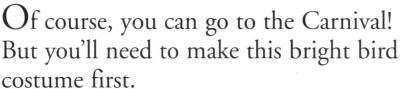 Let's Celebrate!

Of course, you can go to the Carnival! But you'll need to make this bright bird costume first.

MAKING A BIRD MASK

Materials:

- some stiff paper or cardboard
- some shiny or brightly-colored wrapping paper
- felt-tipped pens or paints
- safe scissors
- glue
- a stapler

Directions:

1. To make the bird's head, cut a piece of plain, stiff paper or cardboard into a large rectangle. It has to be big enough to fit your head when it's folded into a cone shape.
2. Color the rectangle with felt-tipped pens or paints if you like.
3. Fold the paper or cardboard into a cone shape. Glue or staple it together.
4. Cut out eye shapes and color them in. Glue them onto the bird's face.
5. Now make the beak. Cut out a triangle and fold it. You can see how it's done in the picture.
6. Now glue or staple the flaps. Stick the beak onto the bird's face.
7. To make the feathers, cut out small rectangles of your shiny or colored wrapping paper. Now cut

each rectangle into thin strips. But don't cut all the way through. You can also cut out feathers with gaps in between.

8. Glue or staple the feathers around the bird's face. Roll one or two of the rectangles up and glue these onto the top of the bird's head.

MAKING A BIRD "COLLAR"

Materials:
- The same materials you used for the head.

Directions:
1. Cut out a paper or cardboard collar to fit around your shoulders — like the one in the picture. Color it in.
2. Make more bird's feathers as you did for the mask.
3. Glue or staple the rectangles of feathers in layers on the collar.
4. When you want to wear the collar, put it around your shoulders. Ask someone to staple it loosely at the back for you.

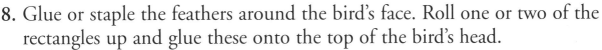

Glossary

angels Spirits who are God's messengers and helpers.

celebrate To show that a certain day or event is special.

celebrations Ways of celebrating a special day, such as parades or parties.

devil An evil spirit who was thrown out of heaven.

confess To own up to something you have done wrong.

fast To give up food, or certain foods, for a set time.

harlequins A playful, funny character in fancy dress.

imps Mischievous spirits.

jesters Jokers.

procession A long line of people walking or dancing along the street.

sins Things we do that are wrong.

theme A particular subject.

tradition A custom; an old way of doing something.

wilderness A deserted, empty place.

Further Reading

Burke, Deidre. *Food and Fasting*. "Comparing Religions" series. Raintree Steck-Vaughn, 1993.

Kelemen, Julie. *Lent Is for Children: Stories, Activities, Prayers*. Liguori Publications, 1995.

Logan, John. *Christianity*. "World Religions" series. Raintree Steck-Vaughn, 1996.

Sandak, Cass. *Easter*. "Holidays" series. Silver Burdett Press, 1990.

Index